# THE 8 ANSWERS

## CONI JUDGE, PhD

Copyright © 2016 by Eden Communication Strategies

All rights reserved. This book or any portion thereof may not be reproduced or used in any manner whatsoever without the express written permission of the publisher except for the use of brief quotations in a book review.

Printed in the United States of America

First Printing, 2016

ISBN-13: 978-1979833707

ISBN-10: 1979833702

www.coni.london

*For today only,
I anger not.
I worry not.
I am grateful and humble.
I do my work with appreciation.
I am kind to all.*

*- Mikao Usui*

# CONTENTS

**Introduction**. . . . . . . . . . . . . . . . . . . . . . . . . . . . . . . . . . . . . . . 1

**#1** Do You Know Where You're Headed? . . . . . . . . . . . . . . . . . . . . 7

**#2** What Makes You Glow? . . . . . . . . . . . . . . . . . . . . . . . . . . . . . . . . 13

**#3** Do You Know How to Be the Boss Without Being Bossy?. . . . . . . . 19

**#4** Do You Know How to Get People to Keep Their Word? . . . . . . . 27

**#5** Do You Hold People Accountable? . . . . . . . . . . . . . . . . . . . . . . . . 33

**#6** What Meetings Do You Actually Need to Have? . . . . . . . . . . . . . . 41

**#7** What Is the Secret to Motivating Staff? . . . . . . . . . . . . . . . . . . . . . 47

**#8** Do You Know How to Get Good Mojo and Keep It? . . . . . . . . . . 53

**Conclusion and Appreciation**. . . . . . . . . . . . . . . . . . . . . . . . . . . 57

# INTRODUCTION

As an owner or manager of a salon, you are the ruler of your own planet. Let's call it Planet Ion—unique, ever-changing, and full of energy. You are the creator and ruler of this planet. You had the dream, found the location and brought your planet to life. You recruited Planet Ionians, your staff who inhabit the planet. There are lots of visitors who come to your new world, your clients. There are other people who help make everything work every day, your suppliers, advisors, friends and family.

Planet Ion is real—hopefully bustling with energy and excitement—and it's yours. But how does it make you feel?

Do you love the planet you've created? Do you look forward to going to Planet Ion every day? Do you like spending time with your team, your clients and the people who make it all come together? Do you feel respected and appreciated as the Supreme Ruler of Planet Ion? Do you feel recharged or exhausted the majority of the time? Does ruling your own world make you happy?

If the answer is "no" or "I'm not sure," you're not alone. Depending on what route you took to become the Supreme Ruler, you may have been more or less prepared for the responsibilities, and, let's face it, the pain in the neck, that being ruler involves. You may have had a vision of what running your own world would be like, but it probably didn't include juggling maternity leaves, holiday requests, broken plumbing, roadwork on your street and finding ways to motivate teenagers and jaded stylists every single day.

It's enough to make a Supreme Leader de-energized and want to take a long trip to a different planet, Planet Cocktail!

I think the reason why so many salon owners and managers struggle with Supreme Leadership is simple: A great leader requires a completely different set of tools from a great stylist. Plus, hairdressing/beauty is a unique industry. So even if you were a successful and happy entrepreneur or leader in another sector, you may find leading Planet Ion a challenge. Instead of recharging you, it can suck the life out of you or at least leave you pretty darn tired at the end of a day, and not in a satisfying "I've worked hard" kind of a way.

In 2010 I started teaching Salon Breakthrough, how-to workshops for salon managers and owners. The amazing salon owners and managers that attend my courses usually have a good sense of business basics like marketing, accounting, managing the books and building a column. The problem is that a lot of them really don't love their world.

I start every workshop by asking, "What do you want from today?" In every workshop at least one person says, "I want to be happier" and "I want to feel passionate about my work again."

# THE 8 ANSWERS TO SALON SUCCESS

As we talk about branding, motivation and other tools to take a salon to the next level, I also keep a list of hot topics that come up. Most of the things that people mention relate to "them," the team at the salon that makes things happen.

- How can I get them to stop sitting in the break room and being lazy?
- Why won't they sell product?
- Why don't they do what I tell them to do? (This is absolutely anything; nothing is too big or too small to turn up on this list.)
- How can I get them to stop doing…? (Again, it's anything: stop former staff from trashing your reputation, stop stealing, stop gossiping, stop people from using too much shampoo, etc.)
- How do I get them to get to work on time?
- How do I keep them motivated and on the same page when there's so much turnover in staff?
- How do I get them to care about my salon as much as I do?

At the end of the day, we go through that list together and think about how to solve each of these problems. Most of the time, I ask questions to get them to think of their own solutions. Questions matter, and if you don't ask them, you're standing still.

This book is a compilation of the questions and answers I think are at the root of why salon managers struggle to become good Supreme Rulers.

The answers aren't revolutionary; they're actually common sense. So when you read them, you're probably going to think two things:

1. I already know this!
2. So why am I not doing it?!

If there's material in here that you already know and do—great! Well done! Keep doing those things because they're your strengths. Make them even stronger.

As for the things you know but aren't doing, ask yourself: Why am I not doing this already?

Being a great leader isn't about what you know; it's about what you do. It's also about knowing your own weaknesses and overcoming them.

Sometimes that means you have to act in a way that makes you feel uncomfortable. Everybody doesn't always love the boss, but they should respect you. In this book I'm *giving you permission to be a Supreme Ruler!* Step up, take the title and rule your world!

If you follow the answers to these eight basic questions for yourself, you'll feel happier, and your team will feel happier. The good news is that knowing the answers makes the action plan pretty straightforward and easy to start doing. You also don't have to work on them all at one time. Skim the book and see what pops out for you. Put the book away and work on one or two things. Then, when you feel you're ready to take another step toward your vision, pull out the book again and work on something else.

## THE 8 ANSWERS TO SALON SUCCESS

If you step up to ask the questions and seek the answers, I guarantee you that your own planet will become a better, happier place to hang out, and it will make more money.

# DO YOU KNOW WHERE YOU'RE HEADED?

The first thing to do is to define success. Supreme Rulers have a vision of their planet, and they have details. You hopefully have a solid business plan so you know you can operate.

This is something bigger. This is full-on, visionary, pie in the sky, if anything were possible what would success look like. Can you answer these questions about your ideal, "perfect" salon, looking ahead two years, five years or 10 years?

1. How much does the salon earn?
2. How big is the salon? (Use any terms you want here, just some sort of gauge it.)
3. How many and what kinds of people work there?
4. What types of clients are you seeing?
5. What's your pay?
6. How are you spending your days most of the time?

7. What three adjectives would describe what your salon looks like, feels like and how it works?

8. What is your salon famous for? (If "famous" doesn't sit well with you, substitute "known for.")

9. What are you, personally, famous for? (Again, swap out "famous" if that triggers a negative response but also think about why you're resisting that word?)

There aren't right or wrong answers. If you want to become world-famous and have the biggest and most successful salon in your area with a huge staff, that's great. If you want to open a whole chain of salons over the next few years, awesome. If you want to have one salon that earns a good living and lets you spend more time with your family, that's cool too.

The key is you have to commit yourself to a destination before you can set the course. If you don't have the coordinates to plug into your career GPS, you'll wander aimlessly and never know whether you've arrived. Without a firm destination, you can't make decisions about where to go when you reach a fork in the road. So you just plod along step by step, day by day, on a road to nowhere. Does that sound energizing or fun? Not so much.

If you know where you're going, you can make decisions. As Supreme Ruler you face either/or decisions every day. Rarely can you have everything you want all the time. Some of these are small decisions: how much stock to buy, who to let go on holiday/vacation, what should I tweet/post today. Some of these are bigger decisions, depending on the size of your business. When you're first starting out, the decisions are actually quite important:

## THE 8 ANSWERS TO SALON SUCCESS

Do I buy a new sofa for reception or do I pay for a photo shoot for a competition? Do I hire a new receptionist or another assistant? Do I want to open on Sundays or do I want to spend that day with my family?

Sometimes, the 'Where am I headed?' questions really stump people. They just won't answer them. If you're resisting answering any of these questions, ask yourself why? It's important to get past this blocker if you want a happy salon.

One salon owner, Alison, just refused to set a personal earnings target. It made her so unspeakably uncomfortable to think about how much money she wanted to pay herself that she was close to an anxiety attack. She could talk about the goals for the salon, her desire to see her salon recognized at Fashion Week and in the industry, but her own salary made her uncomfortable.

If one of these questions is freaking you out, then it's exactly where you need to have an honest conversation with yourself. In this case, Alison had a fear of making money. Not that uncommon, actually. She feared that success would make other people judge her, or she'd alienate friends and family. Without confronting that fear, recognizing that it was real and not ridiculous, she could not fully commit to building a successful salon. If she isn't committed to an outcome, she will never "arrive" and could spend years having an inner turmoil that she didn't really understand.

Now, when Alison gets anxiety thinking about increasing her salary, she can remind herself, "It's okay to make money to provide for myself and my family. I work hard, and I deserve to succeed financially."

## Putting It into Practice

1. After you write down answers to the 'Where am I headed' questions, come up with the first goal you're going to tackle.

> *Example A.* *My goal is to enjoy going to the salon every day.*
>
> *Example B.* *My goal is to increase our turnover by x.*

2. What is the biggest obstacle preventing you from achieving this goal?

> *Example A.* *There always seems to be drama, and it sucks the life out of me.*
>
> *Example B.* *If we don't increase product sales, we can't reach the goal.*

3. What is one thing you can **stop**, one thing you can **start** and one thing you can **continue** doing to overcome obstacles and reach your goal?

> *Example A. I can* **stop** *letting the drama distract me,* **start** *disciplining and possibly get rid of staff with bad energy and* **continue** *hiring people that are a better fit for the salon I want to own and work in.*
>
> *Example B. I can* **stop** *letting under-performers get by with poor sales,* **start** *really focusing on product sales as a top priority and* **continue** *my relationship with my existing product company.*

# WHAT MAKES YOU GLOW?

Have you ever seen a firefly? They dance around in the dark, their little backsides glowing and flickering and they make everything magical. Some shine brighter than others. Well, you're a firefly flying through your life. Sometimes your light is bright, and sometimes it's dim. It depends on the day and what you're doing.

You have to manage your glow. To do this, you need to know what lights you up, what energizes you. And you need to know what sucks the life out of you. If you tap into the energy that lights you up and take action to reduce or eliminate energy depletion, you create a harmony in your life that reinforces and sustains.

Dr. Mihaly Csikszentmihalyi (pronounced "Mike Chick-sent-me-high") first developed the concept called flow. He figured out that when people are working at their best, they seem to do so without effort, like riding a wave of energy. When you're in flow, your glow is recharging itself naturally. You're concentrating on something you love that absorbs you and feels effortless. Time flies by quickly. You can easily tell whether it's going well or going badly so you can readjust. It's not too hard but not too easy, just enough of a challenge to keep you going but not so much that you're overwhelmed. You want to find flow as often as you can in your work because it sustains your glow.

One way to reconnect to your glow is to remember what attracted you to this industry. Why are you in hair/beauty instead of, say, accounting or engineering or dry cleaning? People in this industry are usually artistic, helpful, energetic and personable. They get charged up by thinking about how they can help people or new cool ideas for the future. They like the energy and buzz of a salon. These things recharge them every day and make them glow. Does that sound like you?

If you used to have a glow, and now you don't, it's because your days have changed as a manager/owner:

- Now, instead of spending your days making your clients happy and satisfied, you have to make a whole staff happy and satisfied, and this spreads your glow thin on some days.

- Now, instead of just managing your own column, you have to look at everyone's column, and this adds more stress and makes your glow a little dimmer.

- Now, instead of thinking about when you want to go on holiday/vacation and recharging your glow, you have to think about everyone wanting to go on holiday/vacation at the same time or getting pregnant or quitting or wanting a promotion. This is enough to snuff out your glow entirely.

## THE 8 ANSWERS TO SALON SUCCESS

So, now you're spending <u>less</u> time thinking about the things that <u>recharge</u> your glow:

- Positive relationships
- Making people feel good
- New trends in hair and beauty
- Happy bright future

And you're spending <u>more</u> time thinking about things that <u>drain</u> your glow:

- Details
- Conflict and drama within the team
- Accountants and lawyers
- All the daily numbers

Why isn't the hot water working, and why are there never any clean towels?

The "drainers" will never go away. You can hire someone else to deal with them day-to-day, but as Supreme Ruler you will still have to manage the manager. I'm sorry to tell you this. There is no magic wand to make all that stuff that drains you go away.

But, I am happy to tell you there is a silver bullet. **Manage your glow.**

First, look at your firefly glow and build charging time into every day. Spend as much time as you can doing the things you love.

Second, make a plan to spend less time on the things that drain you without avoiding them. It's tempting to do it later—put off the hard conversations, put off calling the attorney back, put off the things you hate. But if you avoid these things, they will just become a bigger problem and headache down the road.

Keeping your glow glowing is important. **You are the most valuable resource in your salon**. You're more valuable than the most expensive massage chairs, computer system, social media campaign or any other tangible asset. If you don't take care of yourself, you're not being a good Supreme Leader. Taking care of your glow is not being selfish. Taking care of your glow is critical. But glow management requires awareness and sometimes boldness, so you'd best get started.

## Putting It into Practice

1. Think about your goal from number one. What <u>charges</u> or energizes you when you think about that goal? What <u>drains</u> you?

*Example A.*
*<u>Chargers</u>: Enjoying work every day would mean I'm happier. I would probably be more successful and happier in other aspects of my life.*
*<u>Drainers</u>: I don't like the idea of having to get rid of the problem people at the salon. I would have to have some hard conversations I'd rather avoid.*

*Example B.*
*<u>Chargers</u>: Increasing product sales and turnover means a lot more financial breathing room. I could use the cushion to reinvest in the salon and grow.*
*<u>Drainers</u>: I'm not sure I can convince staff to sell, and if they don't sell, I have to follow through on what I said would happen to them. If I focus on product sales,*

## THE 8 ANSWERS TO SALON SUCCESS

*I have less energy and time to focus on other things in the salon, and they could backslide.*

2. Where do you get the most energy from your business now? Ask yourself:

- What specific things do you enjoy doing or love about your work?
- How much time do you spend doing those things now?
- How can you spend more time in energizer mode?
- TIP: *If you're having a hard time thinking of things at work that energize you, expand to think about what energizes you in your life in general? Maybe it's going to the gym, spending time with family or going to movies.*

3. What is sapping your energy now? Ask yourself:

- Who are the people who drain me?
- What worries or concerns are draining me?
- What are the things I avoid doing?
- What can I stop, start or continue to do to minimize the sapping?

4. Think about how you can balance drainers and chargers to reward yourself and stop avoiding the things you don't like doing?

- *If I call the accountant (something that drains me), then I'll take my top-performing stylist to lunch (something that charges me).*
- *After I have a conversation with a staffer that's not performing (drainer), I'll go to the gym (charger).*

# DO YOU KNOW HOW TO BE THE BOSS WITHOUT BEING BOSSY?

Some days being the Supreme Leader (also known as "the boss") really sucks. You probably didn't realize how much it could suck or how often it would suck when you created your planet, did you?

In your vision, your planet had an amazing staff with energy and joy and happy to turn up every day and work hard. Sure, you've worked at salons yourself and seen the haggard and weary look of the salon manager/owner, but your planet would be different. Your planet would be awesome.

And then you opened your salon and opened your eyes. Being Supreme Ruler is hard.

Are you a Supreme Ruler who has completely lost control, and the inhabitants are in charge? Or are you a Supreme Ruler who has had to become a dictator and hates being a dictator?

You want to be a Supreme Leader who is firm and fair, liked and respected. If you aren't this type of Supreme Leader, don't blame the inhabitants for the situation. It isn't their fault. You created a world, established yourself at the head, and now you need to assume command.

This doesn't mean your world has to be boring and no fun. In fact, fun is good. But every party needs a bouncer, or things will get out of hand. You're the bouncer, the one who occasionally has to rain on the parade and have a firm hand. If you don't step up and lead, the partygoers will run amok, and destruction will reign. Then, you'll have no party at all. You don't have to be ruthless as the Supreme Leader, but you do have to step up and have hard conversations and make hard decisions.

## Four Keys to Leading Your Planet and Gaining Respect and Appreciation as Supreme Leader:

1. **Remember you're the Boss.** That means your staff are employees. You are _not_ their friend, confidante, therapist, social director, or hand-holder. You can encourage, develop, champion and support your team. But you're still the Boss. Heed the advice, "If you need a friend, get a dog." Don't make your staff your friends. These people rely on you for a paycheck so they can support their families and themselves, and you rely on them to work so your business can succeed, and you can support your family and yourself. This is the arrangement at the core and why you are both on Planet Ion together. Don't get it confused.

2. **Be brave and face conflict.** Believe in yourself, or at least fake it until you feel it. I work with one manager who always starts by saying, "You know I avoid difficult conversations, so…." I listen to what she's avoiding,

and then I say, "You *believe* you avoid conflict, but you've actually proven you can do it when you need to. So what are your options?"

Is there a hard conversation you're avoiding because you're afraid or just don't want to deal with it? If this is holding you back, use this simple formula to crack the code:

1. Get a piece of paper and write down the person's name, the problem in as few words as possible and the specific day and time you're going to talk to him or her about it.
2. Do it.

If the thought makes you feel slightly ill, think back and remember other times you've had to have tough conversations, and you survived. This won't be the last time you have to face conflict, so accept it and face it and move forward.

3. Never apologize for expecting people to do the job you pay them to do. Did you get that? Let me say it again: <u>Do not, under any circumstances, say "I'm sorry" when you're asking someone to perform a task that you're giving them your hard-earned money to do.</u>

This includes:

- Turning up to work on time
- Staying until it's time to leave
- Giving notice for holidays/vacations
- Washing the towels
- Folding the towels

- Restocking product
- Cleaning the toilets
- Changing the toilet roll
- Sweeping
- Cleaning the dishes in the staff room
- Coming to staff meetings
- Above all, giving your clients good service, a great experience and a flawless result.

Bottom line: The workers on your planet don't decide what the job is. *You* as the founder and Supreme Ruler decide what the job is within reason and in compliance with the law. So, if you decide the assistant's job includes getting your dry cleaning and walking your dog, then that's his job. Be clear, be consistent, be fair, and be in charge. End of story.

When you apologize for asking people do to the job you pay them to do, you imply that they're doing you a favour. **They are not doing you a favour. They're doing their jobs.** You're paying them to do their jobs. So, because this is not a favour, you do not need to beg or apologize.

Supreme Ruler doesn't mean you're a pain, however. You don't need to act like a jerk about it. Usually, salon owners are too nice rather than too mean. So you don't need to say, "Um, when you get time, if you're not busy, do you possibly think you could…?" You're the boss. Talk like one.

**4. Sack people who deserve it.** Your world has a delicate ecosystem. It takes one contagious employee to infect the others with whatever virus they bring to your planet. If it's the high energy/hard worker virus, that's great, but if it's a troublesome virus, that's not so good.

It's good for the Supreme Leader to want to see people succeed, grow and develop. But you cannot give more commitment to someone's success than they give. If he doesn't want to reach his potential, you can't make him, and you're not doing him any favours by letting him get away with bad work. And you really don't want him infecting the others with whatever badness he's bringing to your planet.

If the thought of firing a particular person causes anxiety, think of this: "It's better to have a hole than an a**hole." Sometimes it's scary to think about losing people. But, are you willing to let them hold you hostage? Are they really that valuable and irreplaceable that they can wreak havoc in your salon?

If you're letting a staff member get away with bad behaviour (being late, being "ill" too often, stirring up trouble, etc.) because you're afraid of losing their clientele or being shorthanded, consider this: What message are you sending to those who turn up on time, don't call in sick, are positive and helpful?

You're telling every employee there are no consequences in your salon and how you act isn't important. If you let people get away with murder and hold you hostage, you're Supreme Ruler of a lazy salon infected with the sickness of self-entitlement. You're saying you think it's okay to pay people who can do what they want and when they want, and you don't care enough or aren't strong enough to stop them.

The virus may start small, but it will eventually wipe out the population of hard workers who have committed themselves to your success. So, get rid of the virus. This is hard, but you'll recover. You'll send a clear signal to the entire planet that as Supreme Leader you won't tolerate that kind of behaviour, and you'll take one step closer to having the happy salon you want.

## Putting it into Practice

1. What threatening to infect your salon?

2. What will you do to stop the viruses from spreading? (Think of people who can help, conversations you need to have, systems you can implement, who you need to fire, etc.)

# DO YOU KNOW HOW TO GET PEOPLE TO KEEP THEIR WORD?

You're only as good as your word. The "word" is basically a contract. Sometimes we say it out loud, and sometimes it's just understood and no one needs to say it.

You, as Supreme Ruler, have given your word to your team when you hired them:

- To pay them an agreed amount of money to do a job
- To pay them on time
- To give them a safe and positive environment to work in
- To do your best to have a healthy business that keeps them employed

They, as employees, have given you their word:

- To do the job you hired them to do
- To not take advantage of you (like not stealing) or breaking rules (like arriving late)

So, we're all clear in our hearts and minds about the "Word": These are the promises we made to each other, even if we didn't write it all down in a formal contract. We have a pretty good sense of what's cool and what's not.

We run into a problem when the Word becomes meaningless. The Word becomes meaningless when people start to think it's okay to break the Word and let it slide as long as you have a good enough excuse. *"I'm late because…" "I can't work this weekend because…" "I forgot to do that because…" I need to leave early because…"*

This is how you get a 'Teflon salon"—a place where nothing actually sticks.

The Supreme Ruler is responsible for the Word. You set the example for how you treat the Word in your salon. These are the basics for making the Word strong in your salon:

- **You _must_ keep the Word yourself.** If you break your word, even an implied promise, no matter how big or small, ever, you must acknowledge it and make it right as soon as you can. *"I apologize for being late to the staff meeting today. I know we were to start five minutes ago, but let's get started now."* There's no long drawn out excuse; just acknowledge it and make it right.
- **Be clear on what you're asking people to do.** You do this by following The X by Y Formula:
    - *I need you to (x) fold the towels and put them on the shelf by (y) the end of the day.*
    - *I need you to (x) give a comment card to every client for (y) the entire week.*

## THE 8 ANSWERS TO SALON SUCCESS

- *When you aren't busy, you need to (x) ask Emma what to do (y) right away.*
- *Can you (x) work (y) next weekend?*

When you make it simple, the other person has options. She can say, "Yes, I can do that." She can renegotiate *("I can't do it today, but I can do it first thing tomorrow if that's okay?").* She can commit to commit *("I don't know right now, but can I tell you tomorrow?")* When you make a clear request, and she gives a clear answer, and means it, then you're all good.

- **Give her the option to say no.** This one is a tough sell for some Supreme Leaders. *"But if she says no what will I do?"* My response is, *"Would you rather have her lie and say yes? or say no so you can make an actual plan?"* If people are afraid to say no to you, or if yes is so meaningless that it doesn't even matter, you have a problem with the Word in your salon.

- **Hold her to her word.** If she doesn't keep the Word, you need to call her on it. *"I see you didn't hand out the comment cards to every client this week like I asked. Let's talk about that."* As Supreme Leader, you have a few options about what to do next:

  - *Get her to recommit: "I do need you to (x) hand out the cards to every client (y) next week. Will you commit to do this?"*

  - *Give her a consequence. "I'm going to have to write you up for not doing (x) handing out the client cards (y) this week. It may seem small to you, but it's important to me, and I asked you to do it for a reason."*

  - *Give her a warning. "I need you to (x) hand out the cards (y) next week. If you don't, I'm going to have to write you up."*

## Putting It into Practice

1. Make a list of the requests you're going to make using the X by Y Formula.

2. Think about your own Word. Are you setting the best example in your own life or have you let your Word get sloppy? Who have you broken your Word with? How can you fix your Word with him or her?

# DO YOU HOLD PEOPLE ACCOUNTABLE?

Being really clear and thoughtful about the Word in your salon is a foundation for a happy salon that functions smoothly. But it doesn't really work unless it has substance, and that's where consequences come in. The X by Y Formula has one more element: you need to do (x) by (y) or (z) will happen.

A lot of salon owners have a very emotional and sometimes strong reaction to the C-word—consequences. That's because this is where being Supreme Ruler becomes real. It's a big glow drainer, rarely an energizer. The energy comes after the behaviour that's causing the problem goes away or changes. But to get there, a happier place, you have to hold the line.

Owners/managers usually have a lot to say about the problems in their salons. They can go into great detail about who did what, who said what, what happened, and on and on. But when I ask, "So, what did you do about it?" they get uncomfortable, shift in their chair, stop making eye contact with me and resist answering the question.

Somehow, for a lot of owner/managers, enforcing consequences means being the bad guy. They don't want to be the Supreme Leader who's the bad guy on Planet Ion. They want Planet Ion's inhabitants to just do the right thing without anyone ever having to go to jail, pay a fine, or be banished.

Let's face reality. Life is often about cause and effect. Consequences are a fundamental component that makes our society work. We'd like to think that human decency keeps us on the path of what's right (not stealing, not turning up the music too loud at the party, not speeding) but it's usually because we know there's a consequence, like a fine or jail time, so we restrain ourselves.

If your Planet Ion has no consequences, maybe some people will follow the line because it's the right thing to do. But there are always those who will take advantage and do what's easiest or best for them, simply because they can. And that's not a happy place to live.

Successful salon owners have a handle on the behaviours in their salon. The Supreme Ruler knows what is actually happening, both the stuff they know you see and the stuff they think you don't see. Do they know that you know they sit in the staff room and chat when you're not in the salon? Do they know that you see when they're late? Do they know that you know that they're not recommending products? Not doing the consultation correctly? If they know what they're doing wrong, and they know you know, and they don't care and keep doing it anyway, it's because there are no consequences.

# THE 8 ANSWERS TO SALON SUCCESS

"But how can I make them _____?" is a frustrating question every Supreme Ruler faces. Ideally, people do things because they're asked. You say "will you" and they say "yes," and it's done. Sometimes we need to reward people with bonuses, gold stars, commissions, or pats on the back. But sometimes they won't do things until they see that, if they don't, they will pay a price by taking away something they value. In the salon, what do they value that you control? Their job and their income. This is harsh. This is reality. This is why being the boss isn't easy.

So, is it really that big a deal that they don't hand out the "recommend a friend" card or offer the "product of the week" to every client when you asked them to do it?

If it's a pattern of behaviour, then yes, it is a big deal.

Is it worth being written up, docking pay and possibly getting sacked? Well, yes. There has to be a consequence. If you told them you were going to write them up for being late again, you have to follow through. If you told them you were going to sack them after being late again, you have to follow through.

But prepare yourself. When you try to "kill" or extinguish a behaviour by having consequences, a very powerful and sometimes unpleasant thing happens. Behavioural scientists call this an "extinction burst," and it's not pretty. It means that you're going to see all sorts of "testing" and back-biting and complaining and acting out as soon as the new "consequences" come into play. You have to hold the line. No two ways about it. If you cave in, it will be chaos.

Here's a simple example of a minor extinction burst we can all relate to: You want to watch television. You sit on the sofa, get the remote control, and push the red "on" button. Most of the time the TV switches on, and everything's great. Then, one day, you sit down, get comfy, push the red button, and nothing happens. You press it again. Still nothing. Again. Nada. Then what do you do? The majority of people turn it over and bang the back of the black plastic device, thinking that hitting it will fix it. That's our primal mind reacting to "Why does this thing not work?!" Then our higher mind, the big brain, kicks in and says, "It probably needs a new battery. I'll set it down, not break it, and change the battery." We change the battery, TV works, all is well in the universe, and we move on. But that moment of primal reaction (hitting the black plastic thingy that suddenly stopped working) is our "go-to" default setting. We all have this "bash it" reaction when something changes. Not just with the remote, but we react this way in almost any situation where something we have come to count on suddenly changes.

So when you change the dynamic in the salon and introduce consequences, you become the equivalent of the remote control that doesn't switch on the television anymore. Your team is used to pushing the red button, and you do what you've always done. You say you want something done, they say "okay" and then ignore it, and you pretend it's okay and let it slide or ask nicely again and again.

Now that you're not responding in the same way, instead of letting it slide you actually dock their pay, write them up, or fire them, they react, sometimes violently and powerfully with the emotional equivalent of smacking the remote control (again, you're the remote!). This can take the form of loud complaining, crying, trying to get others to rally against you, refusing to comply, writing awful things on social media, you name it.

Your job is to resist the urge to give in while they're banging. No matter how hard it is and how tired you are, if you suddenly turn "on" while they're still banging, you reward their bad behaviour. You have to wait until they gain sense, activate the big brain and either change their behaviour and comply or decide to leave and go work somewhere else.

So, let's talk through this so you're clear on exactly what needs to happen. No excuses. The Supreme Leader is firm, fair and consistent.

Let's say you've set a clear expectation that *every* stylist is to give a "recommend a friend" card to *every* client on *every* visit; the (x) by (y) couldn't be more clear. The receptionist tells you some staff members, including Sarah, aren't doing it consistently. In staff meeting you tell everyone, "I'm keeping track of the recommendation cards. If you don't hand them out to every client on every visit, I'll write you up." Two weeks later, the receptionist tells you everyone but Sarah is doing it.

You call Sarah in and tell her to sign the written warning. Today. Right this minute. And, if she doesn't (x) hand out the cards to every client for (y) the next week, you will (z) terminate her employment.

How will she respond? Ideally, she'd apologize and start doing it. But the fact that she's choosing to ignore something small means you can probably expect any of the following and more: "It's not fair. Kate doesn't do it either, and you're not writing her up. It's not such a big deal. I'm going to report you."

How do you feel when you read this scenario? Does it make you feel uncomfortable? Do you think it's too harsh? It's just a comment card after all, If you sacked every person who ignored a request, would you have no staff left? So, is it worth the pain?

Yes. It is worth the strife. This can make some salon owners feel really uncomfortable, because it isn't really pleasant. So, *especially* if thinking about the whole (z) part of the equation makes you squirm, you need to *hold the line*. Do not give in. It may be small, and you can think of a thousand reasons and justifications to let Sarah off the hook, but if you're inconsistent, you open the door for bigger things, like theft.

Do not allow people to mess with your money. When you allow someone to negatively impact the profitability of your business, in this case, by blocking a viable way to generate new clients and repeat business, she is not doing "something small," she's taking money out of your pocket. She's making it harder for you to succeed and have a business that employs the entire team. She's being disrespectful and exploiting you. And the rest of your team is watching, sees it, and their trust in you is eroding.

You don't have to justify having consequences. And it doesn't matter whether people think you're being a jerk and unfair. If someone is behaving in a way that you believe is detrimental to your business, you don't have to accept it. Of course, we're not talking about exploiting people or getting them to do things that are illegal or immoral; we all know the line and the law. We're talking about the simple things you need people to do so your business can thrive and holding them accountable.

I guarantee you that the rest of your staff, the ones who are handing out the comment cards, will respect you more for standing up and following through. They will appreciate that you're not letting the slackers slide.

## Putting It into Practice

1. Make a list of consequences you can realistically use when people don't do what you asked them to do. What are your (z)s? Brainstorm every single thing you can think of that's legal, whether it seems reasonable or not. There are only so many levers you can pull but name them all.

2. Now think of these as your "yellow cards" and "red cards" to throw down when someone doesn't follow (x) by (y) requests or otherwise breaks the Word in a serious way. Which ones are "yellow" and which ones are "red"?

3. Don't be afraid to talk to your team about it. Talk to the high performers, the ones who always keep their Word and do what you ask. What do they see as being "reasonable" consequences? You might be surprised that they're even more "hard line" than you are when it comes to consequences.

# WHAT MEETINGS DO YOU ACTUALLY NEED TO HAVE?

Running a world means having meetings. Meetings form the backbone and structure of your salon, but salon managers usually don't like having them and can come up with a dozen excuses for avoiding meetings. If you don't make time to have meetings—with yourself, with your partner, with your advisors, with your suppliers, with your staff—you don't get stuff done.

First, ask yourself what meetings do you need to have and how often? This is a good rule of thumb:

- Partner Meetings/Management Team Meetings— Weekly for 30 minutes, longer once a month.
  - *Objective: Check in to make sure you're on the same page and on track.*
  - *Agenda: What's going well; what's not going well; what should we stop/start/continue doing?*
  - *Make the time! Once a year have a longer meeting to discuss your ideas for the future, the eight questions from the beginning of this book and your goals for the year.*

- **All-Staff Meetings—Monthly Plus a Saturday Morning "Huddle."**
  - *Objective: Everybody on the same page as a team.*
  - *Before: Be clear on what you want them to know, feel and do after the meeting.*
  - *Agenda: Business update; Promotions/Events; Problems/Issues; Requests; Appreciations (See #7 "Say Well Done" below.)*

- **Key Staff One-on-One Catch-ups—As Needed.**
  - *Receptionist—Daily or weekly*
  - *Manager/key stylists or colourists—weekly or monthly*
  - *Each key staff member—monthly*

- **Supplier/Advisor Meetings—Monthly/Quarterly/Annually.**
  - *Who do you rely on to make your salon work? Depending on the size of your salon, it could include your accountant, lawyer, marketing/PR, social media/website manager and others.*
  - *Objective: Make sure things are moving in the right direction. Have a longer meeting once a year to agree on the bigger plan and your objectives.*

Having good meetings with the right people at the right time makes all the difference. This means you need to put the time in the diary and make sure they happen, but you also need to **make a plan to have a good meeting.**

## Before the meeting:

- **Have an agenda**. Write down on a piece of paper what you want to talk about *before* the meeting. Every meeting. Every time.
- **Know the point.** What do you want to decide, move forward, or get out of this meeting?
- **Invite the right people.** Are the right people in the room to achieve the objective? Do you need to include someone else so the meeting will be as productive as possible? (For example, if you want to have a meeting with a supplier to reduce costs, do you need to include a senior stylist who knows what's selling and what's not? If you're having a meeting with your marketing person, do you need to have the receptionist there to give input?)

## During the meeting:

- **Start and stop on time.** Show respect for those who are giving their time and be punctual. If the meeting is to end at 3:00, but you've got more to cover, at 2:55 say, "We're meant to end in five minutes. Can we carry on a little longer or should we set another meeting to finish this up?"
- **Agree to the objective with everyone.** "We're going to cover this." or "This is what I want us to achieve in this meeting." Ask if there's anything else they want to cover so you can allow time.
- **Stay on track.** If the meeting goes into a random direction, say "That's a good point. Let's discuss it another time and I'll write it down to make sure we don't forget."

- **Make it stick**. At the end of *every* meeting agree: Who is doing (x) what by (y) when?
- **Make it positive.** I end every meeting by saying thank you and sincerely telling the person what I appreciate about them. It doesn't need to be cheesy, just simple and sincere. Supplier: "I appreciate you caring about my business like it was your own." Partner: "I appreciate that we're in this together, and we can talk openly about things." Staff: "I appreciate you taking the time to be here and be part of this team." At the end of every staff meeting, leave a few minutes to go around the circle and have each person tell one other person what they appreciate about them, something simple like "I appreciate Ryan for rinsing my colour and taking his break later." We'll talk more the power of positivity in the next step.

## After the meeting:

- **Make sure everything you've agreed on gets done.**
- **Make sure everyone knows what they're supposed to do**. I'm a big fan of the "post meeting email" or note on the bulletin board or your staff Facebook page that just says: "Thanks for meeting today. I wrote down that we're going to do these things: If I've missed anything or you have a question, let me know. Thanks!" Easy peasy.

## Putting It into Practice

1. Make a list of the meetings you need to start having and put them in the diary/calendar. Now.

2. If you have to cancel a meeting, reschedule it immediately. Don't procrastinate, or it won't happen.

3. If you keep cancelling the same meeting, stop and think why you're not making it happen? What are you avoiding? Is it a subject you feel uncomfortable with or a person who's sucking the life out of you so you avoid the meeting? If it's the subject, remind yourself of why it's important to tackle it head on. If it's a person, can you replace them (in the case of a vendor/supplier) or is there someone else you can ask to pick up the relationship and report back to you (like have your salon manager meet with the receptionist weekly so you don't have to.)

# WHAT IS THE SECRET TO MOTIVATING STAFF?

Being a respected and appreciated Supreme Leader isn't for the faint of heart. If this feels difficult and unfamiliar, remember you'll need some time to really get a handle on it. You may make mistakes. That's expected. It's okay.

The good news is that one of the most important things you can do to have a happy salon is going to come more naturally to you and feel like fun, and that's celebrating when people do good work. Have a party for the ones who do the job, do it well and are on the team.

It's super-easy to have a great vibe in your salon every day if you make a point to give positive comments and encourage appreciation. (See #6 in the "meetings" section where you end every meeting by telling the team what you appreciate and having them tell each other what they appreciate about their teammates.)

Let's start with appreciation. It's simple. What do you appreciate about the person—big or small? The only rule about appreciation is that it needs to be sincere, not just words. It's better to have one real appreciation that's small ("I appreciate you bringing me a coffee today. Thanks.") than to have big meaningless generic statements. Set the example and build a team that's appreciative, and you'll see a transformation in your salon.

Next is to build your positivity muscle by using the 5:1 rule. This means making FIVE positive comments for every ONE negative statement or criticism—every single day. It's a challenge, but you can do it.

Need inspiration? Here's a list of things to say:

1. Good work.
2. Well done.
3. You did a lot of work today.
4. It's a pleasure to work with you.
5. Great job.
6. That's right.
7. Nice going.
8. That's coming along really well.
9. That's great.
10. Let's do that.
11. Excellent.
12. Good job.
13. Exactly right.
14. You're on target.
15. Good thinking.
16. Wonderful.

17. That's good.
18. You've worked hard on this.
19. That's it.
20. Let's share this with others.
21. Good for you.
22. You're learning fast.
23. You did well today.
24. Keep up the good work.
25. I'm glad your approach is working.
26. Good solution.
27. That's better than ever.
28. You've figured it all out.
29. You've got it.
30. Very resourceful.
31. Good progress.
32. I like that.
33. I couldn't do it better myself.
34. Now that's what I call a great job.
35. You did that very well.
36. Outstanding.
37. Keep up the great work.
38. That's wonderful.
39. You mastered that in no time.
40. Congratulations.
41. You make our work fun.

42. I'm glad I assigned you to this.

43. You showed great leadership.

44. I knew I could count on you.

45. You made a difference.

46. You have my complete support.

47. Clever idea.

48. I'm glad you're on our team.

49. Thank you.

50. Very good.

## Putting It into Practice

1. End every staff meeting with an appreciation. Everyone participates, even the ones who roll their eyes and act as if it's stupid. It will feel awkward and weird at first, and then people will start remembering things, and it will make a huge difference.

2. Appreciate yourself. How often do you stop and tell yourself you did a good job? If you don't appreciate yourself, you can't appreciate others. So, look at the list above, insert your name when you talk to yourself as Supreme Ruler of Planet Ion, and every day remember to tell yourself what you appreciate whether it's work-related or not: "Self, I appreciate you for sticking to your guns today when it was hard." or "Self, I appreciate you for taking the time to eat a good lunch today."

3. Get a "positivity" monitor and make a game of the 5:1 ratio. If you say something negative, remember it and then come up with five positives. The salon is on-board, and you can explain this is something you want to do because you want a happy salon and a GREAT PLACE TO WORK!

# DO YOU KNOW HOW TO GET GOOD MOJO AND KEEP IT?

**It's simple:**

- Share your success
- Be generous
- Give back

Supreme Leaders don't get respect and appreciation without the help of others. So think about who has supported you and who needs your support.

I want you to close your eyes and visualize two people:

1. A person who made a huge difference in your life. Someone who saw things in you that you didn't see in yourself. Someone who helped get you on a path to success.

2. A person you know you can help by "passing on the fire" you received. Make a promise to yourself to help this person without telling them that's what you're doing.

By visualizing these two, real, unique, specific individuals, you can (1) thank and honour the person who believed in you, while (2) promising to do the same for someone else.

This is a powerful place to be as a Supreme Ruler of your own, happy, smooth-functioning salon because it helps you see the bigger picture. It helps you reignite the flame that made you start in the first place.

Go back to the questions you answered in the beginning. What do you want to be famous for? Another way of saying that, is, "What do you want to be remembered for." This is your higher purpose, your own big picture. When you're pursuing your higher purpose and giving back along the way, you have passion and energy and are happy.

The need to make a difference is part of your DNA. Connect to your team. Connect to your clients. Focus on being a great boss. Focus on providing a valued service. Notice how you help others and how others help you.

## Putting it into Practice

1. Shut the door. Sit down. Put on some music. Get three sticky notes and a pen:
    a. Close your eyes and force yourself to think about the person who has supported you. See his or her face. Remember how it felt to know someone believed in you. Open your eyes and write that person's name on the sticky note right now.

b. Now, close your eyes and force yourself to think about one person you could make a difference for going forward. It may be someone who works for you or someone in your personal life. See him or her in your mind. What are you going to do, big or small, that they may not even see or know about that will make a difference? Open your eyes and write that person's name down on a second sticky note.

c. Finally, close your eyes and step out of yourself. Fast forward five, 10, 15 years, whatever makes sense for you. What are the three words you want people to think of when they think about you? Write those three words down on your last note.

2. Stick these notes on your desk, in a notebook, or put them in a drawer. This is what it's about—making a difference and being your best self.

# CONCLUSION AND APPRECIATION

I wrote this book because I believe hairdressers and salon owners have one of the hardest jobs in the world, and are often under-appreciated. Whenever I hear a stylist say, "I'm *just* a hairdresser," I think "What a shame you don't see how important you are."

The bottom line is the salon owners who succeed and become amazing Supreme Leaders don't do it by accident. They're purposeful, focused and committed. They care. *And, there's nothing they can do that you can't do too.*

Over the years I have had the fortune to meet, get inspiration from and work with some amazing salon owners and industry thought leaders who helped me realize this book was important to write and I should lead by great example.

Thank you to every salon owner, manager and stylist who ever attended one of my courses or workshops and are brave enough to share their stories and kind enough to listen to mine. I appreciate their insights, examples and support. I give great appreciation to my mentors and thinking partners who planted seeds. And thanks to the best salon assistants I've ever met (and raised), Ryan Judge and Connor Judge.

www.ingramcontent.com/pod-product-compliance
Lightning Source LLC
Chambersburg PA
CBHW050020230526
45470CB00003B/1059